KU-497-449

RIVERS, MOUNTAINS and DESERTS

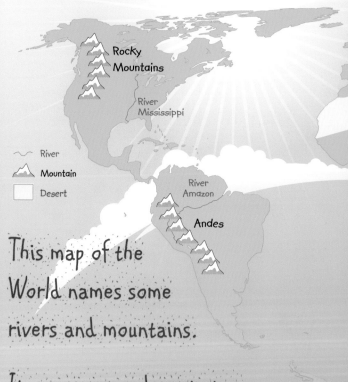

Rocky Mountains

River Mississippi

S

River
Amazon

Andes

River

Mountain

Desert

This map of the World names some rivers and mountains.

It names some deserts too.

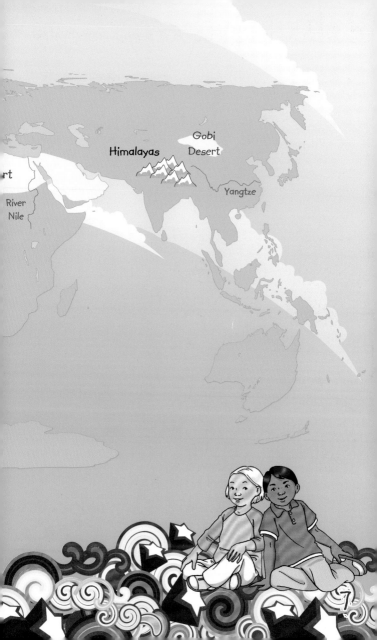

Himalayas

Gobi
Desert

Yangtze

rt

River
Nile

CONTINENTS and OCEANS

Arctic

North
America

Atlantic
Ocean

This map shows

continents

South
America

and oceans.

Pacific
Ocean

Atlantic
Ocean

The huge areas of land

are called continents.

The huge areas of water are called ocean

8

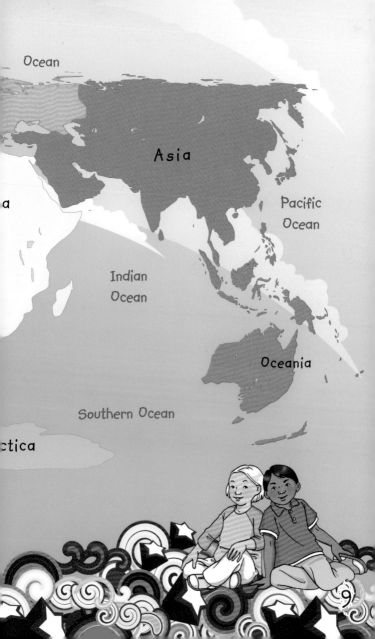

Ocean

Asia

Pacific
Ocean

a

Indian
Ocean

Oceania

Southern Ocean

ctica

9

NORTH AMERICA

North America is the
third largest continent.

The highest mountains
are called the
Rocky Mountains.

Nor
Amer

The biggest country
in North America
is Canada.

The biggest city is
New York.

SOUTH AMERICA

South America
is smaller than
North America.

So
Ame

The longest river
in South America
is the Amazon.

Most of the people
speak Spanish
or Portuguese.

EUROPE

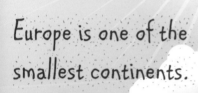

Europe is one of the smallest continents.

Europe has many small countries and large cities.

E

Some parts of
Europe are very cold
or wet in winter.

e

15

AFRICA

A

Africa is the second largest continent.

The River Nile is in Africa. It is the longest river in the world.

The Sahara Desert
is in Africa.
It is the largest
desert in the world.

ASIA

Asia is the largest continent in the World.

The world's highest mountain is in Asia. It is called Mount Everest.

18

The longest river
in Asia is the
Yangtze.

Tokyo is the biggest
city in Asia.

OCEANIA

Oceania is made up of Australia, New Zealand and many small islands.

Many of these islands are surrounded by coral reefs.

O

ia

The Great Barrier
Reef, near the coast
of Australia, is the
biggest in the world.

COUNTRIES and CITIES

U
Lond

New York

U.S.A.

Los Angeles

Nigeri

Brazil

Buenos Aires

There are many countries and cities in the World. Some of the countries and big cities are named on the map.

Moscow

Russian Federation

Cairo

Beijing

China

Japan

India

Tokyo

Mumbai

Kenya

CapeTown

Australia

Sydney

Let's visit some countries.

U.S.A.

New York

Washington

The United States of America is in North
America. It is made up of fifty states.
The biggest city is New York.
The capital city is Washington.

BRAZIL

Brasília

São Paulo

Brazil is the largest
country in South
America. São Paulo
is the largest city.
Brasília is the
capital of Brazil.

25

INDIA

Himalayas

New Delhi

India is a country in Asia. Part of the world's highest mountain range is found in India. It is called the Himalayas.

London

The United Kingdon is a country in Europe. It is surrounded by water. The biggest city in the United Kingdom is London.

KENYA

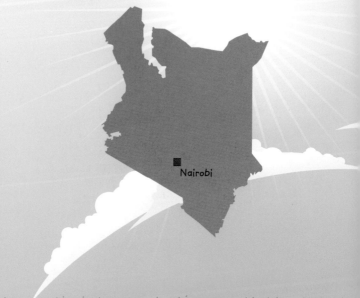

Nairobi

Kenya is country in Africa. It has lots of sunshine all year round. Nairobi is the capital of Kenya.

Sydney

Canberra

ustralia is the largest country in
ceania. It is a huge island. The largest
ity is Sydney.

CHINA

Beijing

China is in Asia. It is a huge country .
Over a billion people live in China.
Beijing is the capital of China.